STUM1

THE LIGHT

will show up on the 29th

5 Questions (of this book to her) Typed

- writes a lof informs

Antrim House

STUMBLING INTO
THE LIGHT

Poems by

Edwina Trentham

Antrim House

Printed in the United States of America

Library of Congress Control Number: 2004111720

ISBN 0-9662783-8-0

First Edition

2004

Cover: frieze panel from Vézelay Cathedral
Photo by courtesy of Auguste Allemand
Book Design: Caitlin Snyder and Rennie McQuilkin
Book Production: EPS Printing, South Windsor, CT

Antrim House
www.antrimhousebooks.com
860.217.0023

ACKNOWLEDGEMENTS

Grateful acknowledgement to the editors of the following publications, in which these poems first appeared, sometimes in earlier versions:

The American Scholar: "Sunday Night"

Chester Jones Foundation National Poetry Competition Winners Collection: "My Mother Remembers Clothes" (1990), "My Mother and the Baby's Breath" (1994)

The Denny Poems: "Two Houses" (1983), "Keeping Secrets" (1984)

Embers: "Snake Song"

The Massachusetts Review: "My Father's Gift"

Pivot: "Homing," "In Bermuda, Narcissus Grows Wild," "Scarecrow"

The Poetry Miscellany: "Freeze Frame"

Poets On: "Sea Urchins"

Red Fox Review: "Talking to Mr. Lopez"

Scintilla: "Calling My Father By Name"

Thanks to Yaddo for the gift of time, during which some of these poems were written or revised.

Finally, there are no words powerful enough to express my gratitude to Tony Connor—extraordinary teacher, mentor, and friend—who was the first one to believe in my work. He changed my life.

For Greg and Ben

STUMBLING INTO THE LIGHT

CAST OUT

SOLACE

WATER DEEPLY CLOSE TO DARKNESS

STUMBLING INTO THE LIGHT

Be not afeard. *The isle is full of noises,*
Sounds, and sweet airs that give delight and hurt not.
Sometimes a thousand twangling instruments
Will hum about mine ears, and sometimes voices
That if I then had wak'd after long sleep
Will make me sleep again; and then in dreaming
The clouds methought would open and show riches
Ready to drop upon me, that when I wak'd
I cried to dream again.

—William Shakespeare, *The Tempest*

Love is a stone
that settled on the sea-bed
under grey water.

—Derek Walcott, "Winding Up"

CAST OUT

BEACH SONG

Come with me. I know the way
to the beach
better than anyone, know just where
bay grapes drop their purple-skinned
sweetness onto green-plate leaves

barely a step from the place
where the turquoise sea unfolds
a sheet of pink sand
scattered with waterbottles—pale grapes
full of seasalt, cold enough to
wake the grownups.

Come. My father is there, too thin,
my mother too
beautiful—and down where the waves
sweep and tumble our feet
my sister and I still sit, arms entwined,
watching the sea
coming and going forever.

PHOTOGRAPH

The early evening sun, faded to pale
sepia with the passing years, touches
our faces with a soft glow, and reaches
past us to scatter shadows on the hill.
Side by side, with freshly washed hair and clean
pajamas, we sit on the stone wall by
my mother. She leans forward, her eyes
shining with a smile for someone unseen,
while my sister, elbows on knees, small chin
cupped, gravely imitates her graceful pose,
which I, barely three, try to reproduce
by splaying my fingers, clutching my face,
so I can mirror my sister's sad eyes.
It is wartime, and on the back, written
in pencil, are the words *See how we've grown*—
for my father, away for a year by then.

THE SHORT WAY TO THE BEACH

Dust and grass, the path is lined with fennel, the sky
cloud-scrimmed, and the cows stand, chew their cud,
eyes moving with us. The beach is too far this way.

We straddle the fence, pause, then without a word
drop to the other side and saunter—swinging brown
bags and bathing suits—single file, gazes hard

fixed fifty yards ahead. I watch your hair bob down,
up, down, count my steps, and pretend I don't see
the one who moves steadily toward us, like none

of the others. I taste brass in my throat, a sigh
bubbles to my lips, and I can feel the thick
muscle of his out-thrust neck, smell his rough hide,

wait only for his horns, curved like a heart, to prick
the soft backs of my thighs, as we break stride, and I
scramble the fence behind you, falling to the rock

strewn pathway that leads us to the beach and safety—
the crash, hush of the bright green, miraculous sea.

NANNY

The walls of the buttery
are slatted, the cold stone floor
striped dark and light where you squat,
unrepentant. Privileged child,
I carry empty garbage
pails up the steep hill, linger

near the match-me-if-you-can,
lids clashing allegiance, wait
for the comfort of your tapped
defiance. But Nanny is
already there, lips flattened
around wooden pins, snapping

a sheet to warn me back. Late
afternoon spills blue shadows
when you emerge, and we sit
side by side at the kitchen
table while I eat for both
of us, to please her, wait for

the years to pass, so you can
tell me how you fell to your
knees, and about the bright crash
of cymbals, the white robe's harsh
slap—about knowing at once
it was Nanny's God, come just

as she had promised He would
to strike you dead.

SOUVENIR

When our father came back—bringing Persian
beads the bottomless blue of our own skies—
you fed the next door neighbors' child silver
spoonfuls of dirt, holding him fast between
your knees like a fiercely loving mother,
while the cows switched flies and shifted their great
haunches beneath the cedars' shadow. Who
can remember which one of us scurried
home for the necklace—sifting the clutter
of reunion for its bright azure coil,
then stumbling down the hill, beads clicking cool
on warm skin—although I know you straddled
the splintered fence and called the russet neck
closer, then watched the gentle sway of blue
disappearing in the flowered meadow.

CAST OUT

Two days, my mother tells me, and *we'll be
gone.* She doesn't tell me where. Behind me
on the shadowed porch, the grownups
clink glasses. Beyond flat
gravel paths, below the long
green lawn, the sun beats silver
into the sea. The tricycle seat
burns my bare thighs, burns through
my thin cotton underpants,
my palms are sticky on black
rubber. I grip hard, lean forward, to push
one pedal—brake—lean back. Back and forth,
back and forth, elastic pinching the soft
flesh under my arms. All their backs
are turned. Now.

I am thumping,
clattering,
spilling down the wide
steps, for an instant
flying free,
then smashing
my brow into blood
and stones, sprawling,
becoming one
with the bright indifference
of the insects' song.

MY FATHER'S HEART

I was seven, I think, when the carving knife's thin
blade sliced my finger through the dishtowel, sliced right
to the bone it seemed, as I watched the white cloth turn
crimson, tasted a rush of bile, choked on my breath
at the sweet, sticky smell of blood, then whimpered once,
like a scampering puppy who skids and catches

its foot in a slammed door. I raised my hand to catch
my mother's eye, but I was not surprised the thin
knife had found my finger. I knew better, or once
I saw that eager blade I did, so she was right
to be furious, to glare and suck in her breath,
to twist the towel tight to staunch the blood, then turn

me roughly, hustle me, with one impatient turn
back to snap the light off, rush me outside to catch
a cab, whistle it down, stare ahead, me breathing
hard against tears, she smoking, lecturing, voice thin
with anger. But all that vanished the next day, right
after breakfast, when my father, home just this once

because of a snowstorm, took me sledding—the one
and only time he did—and when I tried to turn
the sled, held the rope too hard, cried out, he was right
there, saw my blue mitten leaking red, and caught
me in his arms, to run me home. Oh, his long, thin
legs plowing us through the heavy snow, his quick breath

coming in smoky puffs in the clear air, his breath
echoing the sound of his strong heart thumping, once
he hit his stride, and oh my head against his thin
chest, bumping in time to his footsteps. When I turn

to this memory, that's where I choose to stay, caught
up in those few moments, the way my ear was right

against his beating heart, how he carried me right
home through the snow, in his arms. I catch my breath
at this point. The truth is, details have never caught
up with longing in this story. I thought, just once
I'd like to see what happened next, see how it turned
out, but I won't shape memory to fit some thin

version of truth, wrest one right story from scatters
of desire—thin stuff when I can just turn back,
find myself caught up, held still in love's sweet breath.

FREEZE FRAME

The orange-throated tiger
lilies fly past my feet. Crouched
on the running board, I cling

close to my father's profile,
watch his hands twist the leather
steering wheel to bring me home

safely up the rutted drive.
His shadowy silhouette,
head thrown back to drink

from the tilted gin bottle,
is still years away, somewhere
in the sun splattered future—

an island where black men sweep
the roadside, collecting heaps
of bruised trumpet flowers, dead

toads grown brittle in the heat
of summer, like old wishbones
left hanging too long to dry.

KEEPING SECRETS

That was the summer Aunt Kitty decided
to paint her toenails black—curving her back white
by the shadowed swimming pool, while my sister
hunched on the far side, paddling her feet, watching.
The day she finally caught them together,
sun slicing through half-drawn curtains, she turned

her face from the curve of pale shoulders turning
gold in shafts of light, stood undecided
as my father reached fumbling hands to gather
his clothes around him, smoothing the sheet's white
turmoil with a mutter of lies. Watching
Aunt Kitty was a passion for my sister

from then on. And for Aunt Kitty, my sister's
devotion was a prize—a love that might turn
sour at any time, and so must be watched,
wooed with toenail polishes (they decided
rose was best) and the discarding of thick white
cotton for lacy underpants bought together

on shopping sprees. Such attention, together
with my mother's homecoming, drove my sister
into hiding, and she watched behind starched white
curtains in relief when Uncle Charles returned
for Aunt Kitty. Who knows why she decided
not to tell—certainly no one was watching

her anymore. Though soon she started watching
my father when they were alone together—
perplexed, as if waiting for him to decide
what they remembered. Finally my sister

24

simply chose to become unlovable, turned
away from him, weaving a curtain of white

lies and good manners between them. Today, white
with pain, she tells me: *He was always watching
me—wouldn't forget. Can't you see how he turned
from me?* In their last picture together,
my father reaches back to help my sister
from her bridal carriage. She is deciding,

curving her white back to look, how to gather
her skirt. The camera watches while my sister
turns her face away from him, undecided.

SOLACE

THE WAY THE DARK OPENS OUT
INTO LIGHT

-i-

This is home, I tell myself, naming the past
five years *away* for the first time, holding fast
to the ship's mahogany rail, as we plow through
emerald shifting sapphire. Our wake spills foam
onto the shore, close enough for me to see
the way dead cedars web the green with gray, close
enough to name the yellow, *frangipani,*
name the purple, *bougainvillea,* to recall
that lawn where I was banished once to search for
my lost hair ribbon, where I named the spider
shadows *oleander, poinciana,* while
my mother's beautiful laughter poured silver
out of the open window, and the roof glared
white underneath a frozen sheet of moonlight.

-ii-

The water shivers blue with angel fish,
darts with yellow grunts, but today a shark
has the harbor, so I'm walking the black
coral to toughen my feet. I squat near
pools of trapped fry to let the hermit crabs
pin-scuttle my palms, slide cool needles
of casuarina between my fingers,
and bite hard on the berries to pucker
my mouth. When midday turns the sea to brass,
I find the back of the house, its walls dark
with damp, thick with moss, breadfruit rotting sweet
into its roots, where dried banana fronds
shift and split underneath my feet, bleeding
still from my first day back in paradise.

If I breathe deeply enough, the hammock
will sway, and when I squint into the blue
afternoon, I can make the sky dissolve.
My mother says a new friend is waiting
for me next door, but I know the pathway
is one long shadow, where spider lilies
lean to brush my thighs, and each step freezes
a fern-green chameleon, an orange fan
flicking at its throat. And I know the way
the dark opens out into light again,
the way the path hugs the cliff, the bright sea
whispering just to my left. One foot wrong,
and I'm over, a scream caught by the air
then swallowed by a white scatter of foam.

THE HARBOR

The two sisters are lying belly down
on inflatable mattresses, the tips
of their noses just touching the water's
clear surface. They are counting angel fish,
yellow grunts, cowpollies—shimmers of blue
and gold scattered with the minnows' silver
arrows that come and go beneath their drifting
shadows. In early morning, the harbor
is an emerald shot through with light, broken
by rocky islands and jutted with small
stone docks, the sky that impossibly pure
blue of the tropics, scattered with thin clouds,
seabirds soaring to catch the wind, hanging
an instant, then floating to bright water.

The sisters lie here for hours each day,
contemplating their luck, their parents' luck
in having rich friends who let them summer
in this huge house, where there's room to sidestep
their unpredictable mother, the blaze
of her laughter and its chilly shadow,
to avoid the soft chink of glass on glass,
as their father waters the gin. They've learned
to make their way alone in paradise,
and so, the morning they hear of the shark
in the harbor, are told by someone *Stay
out of the water for now,* they simply
haul themselves onto the stone dock, scraping
their sunburned knees, pull the wet mattresses

after them, then sit quietly, thin arms
wrapped tightly around their chests, shivering

just a little as their hair drips slowly
down their necks and their salty backs begin
to dry to itching. Scanning the broad
sweep of green, they squint the sun away, note
the innocent shift and surge of waves sent
shoreward by passing ocean liners. When
the *all clear* comes, they glance up at the house,
its closed shutters, and turn to each other,
imagining those blank eyes, that white smile
gliding just below the harbor's sun-splashed
surface. Then, shifting slightly for comfort,
they hunker down to wait until they're sure.

TWO HOUSES

We shared the wide verandah,
a clear sweep of sky filtered
through a yellow-striped awning,
and a love of words. Listen:

say *a-bomb-in-a-bull*;
the plural of *octopus*
is *octopodes*; and, yes,
il faut souffrir pour être belle.

The garden rose behind us
in flowered terraces, fine
raked, strewn with charcoal. I dug
for it, drew slender horses

and one laughing girl after
another for my father.

In the winter house our lives
divided. Still, there were days
when I stayed sick at home, listened
to the battered gate creaking

his return from morning walks,
his slow steps moving to greet
the postman, the afternoon's
shrill call to tea—while I swayed

in the hammock left behind
in the summer garden, sweet
with waxen stephanotis
and spiky passion flowers,

and dreamed of being with him
until the end of my life.

TALKING TO MR. LOPEZ

Mr. Lopez crouches, tugs the thin
white streams into a smudged glass, offers
it with a smile. I drink, thanking him,
obregado, as my father does.

At Easter Mr. Lopez offers
me a pair of wry-necked baby chicks.
I name them Noel and Mary, for
my parents, and fall in love with their

helplessness, do not anticipate
their transformation to a mottled
frenzy of scaly legs and frantic
beaks, am too soon helpless in the face

of their shrill insistence. I begin
to dream of silence, keep seeing them
dead. Until one morning I press my face
to their cage, discover they have pecked

each other's eyes out. There is no one
I can tell, but all day long I see
myself returning the blinded chicks,
murmuring *obregado* over

and over, rolling each syllable
on my tongue the way my father taught me.

BRUISING

Alone in the shadowed kitchen,
she peels the peach, tearing
at its warm, rosy skin with eager
fingers, pushing deep to find

bruises, willing her thumb
to bury itself in that one
soft spot she knows is there,
so she can feel it—that cold

rush of relief—and revel in the lonely
delight of spoiling, in being
the first to sense the fruit
is turning, the first to toss it out.

SEA URCHINS

Sea eggs, we used to call them, diving
deep to lift them from rippled
underwater sand, cupping our hands
to balance the dark needles

on our tender palms, then lining them
up on the dock's hot stone face
to dry, until the spines fell away
in drab little heaps, hoarding

the stench of low tide. And when at last
the shells emerged, in hollow
curves of lavender, we tossed them back,
a slow spiral through turquoise

to the cool ocean floor. Until one
time, when the water grew still,
I stretched face down on the sunburned dock
and watched their silence, lying

there for an hour or more, holding
my eyes just above water,
and suffered heatstroke. For days I lay
in darkness, dreamed all my flesh

had seared away and left me
a husk, so perfect, so terrible
that I prayed for mercy in my sleep.

SUNDAY NIGHT

The upstairs bathroom is cold, but I can lie
stretched out, full length, at fourteen, still shy
three inches of the tub's six feet, square bones
of my knees poking just above the water, drops
spangling my flat belly. I hear my sister thudding
up the stairs, the crash of her slamming bedroom
door, my father's deep voice a floor below,
distant as summer rain on the limestone roof.

Against my closed eyelids my sister hunches,
smoking, sobbing, staring out at the sweep
of dark sea, cursing my father for not loving her,
my mother for not loving anyone. I sniff hard
to catch one more whiff of that Easter Lily
perfume I scattered across the water's clear
surface, then reach with my right foot to grip
the tap with my toes, flip the hot water

into a thin steady stream. Steam rises, floats,
fogs the room, coats the mirror. Tomorrow
in school, my skin will smell like flowers.

WAITING TO CHANGE

The day after I found the chameleon, lost
in the bathtub—gray-green waiting to change
to ivory—my sister fainted behind
the bathroom door, sprawled on the floor, cold
deaf for ten minutes. Strange that I recall both
these events, when all that matters is the closed

door, the way my sister was always closing
doors, slamming into her shuttered bedroom, lost
in rage at our father when their fights left both
of them dumb, while I watched, practiced changing
to a shadow, losing myself in that cold
hallway. By day, I hid my terrors behind

a smile, but I must have hoped she hid love behind
those bursts of fury, because at night her closed
door called to me, and I would crouch by the cold
pencil of light at the bottom, like a lost
cat, scratching gently, praying she would change
her mind and take me in, pretend we were both

afraid. Twice she let me share her bed, and both
times I huddled the wall while she lay behind
me in the airless dark, curled away, unchanged,
swallowing her anger, until the close
room filled with my ragged breath. Then she lost
her patience, turning over and hissing cold

on my neck, *Stop breathing,* turning colder
when I whispered, *Don't be angry,* until both
of us were lying like twin statues, lost
in these impossible demands, one behind

the other, while I tried to keep my lips closed,
sipping at the air. Finally her changed

breathing would set us free, and I could change
my position, push myself away from the cold
wall and carefully twine myself closer
to my sister, breathing with her, until both
of us grew warm, and the flickering behind
my eyelids turned to sleep. But in that lost

time closest to dawn, my sister always lost
her warmth, turning colder than the wall behind
me, changing us both back into stone again.

FALLING

My seventeenth summer is mostly spent
on an island, babysitting. He's young,
the father who ferries me back in late
afternoon, the two of us alone, face

to face in that little boat—he with his faded
blue shirt, sun-brown neck, me with hands clasped
between my thighs, spray cool on my cheeks when
I turn to see how far I am from home, the thrust

of bristled coral where my father waits
to fend off. The last day I whisper *Bill*—
trying it on my tongue as the boat pulls
away—turn around at my father's cry,

just in time to see him fall, just too late
to catch him. Because he saw it, the jut
of my hip, how hard I hugged myself
as I turned from him to wave goodbye.

IN BERMUDA, NARCISSUS
GROWS WILD

The fields of memory are sweet
with jonquils, starry white blossoms, bent
double in the thin rain of early
spring. I gather pale clusters to pin
in my hair for the RNO's dance
the year I turn seventeen. We're on
the list, my sister and I—pretty
faces, good families—the island's
best, picked out beforehand, then gathered
whenever the Royal Navy sends
its officers ashore—white hats
tucked underneath their arms, gold wedding
rings in their pockets—to touch our sweet,
our unfamiliar hearts.

My mother chaperones, watches me
dance, white-faced, lit up with my new-found
power. She will wait almost thirty
years to talk about the friend who takes
her aside, whispers, *Stand back, Mary.*
Let your daughters have their chance. Only
then will I recall how her laughter
spilled at my sister's uneasy stance
in her first high-heels; the way she bent
her head to tell me she wasn't sure
after all about my dress—*all those*
buttons; and how the light near her bed
fell hard on her face when I came home
triumphant, terrified.

THE SUMMER I DECIDE WHO I AM

-i-

Just eighteen, out of school, I am painting
scenery, apprentice in a summer
theatre—gray splotched on plasterboard—making
sixteenth century cottages: Shakespeare,
transformed to Prospero, calls forth the wind.
Stratford dissolves to the *still-vex'd Bermoothes.*
Ariel appears, disappears behind
a cedar tree. As he moves, his voice moves,
while Caliban, in loud Bermudian,
cries to dream again. Promoted to sound,
flipping microphones, I am in heaven.
This is who I am: Miranda, one hand
on her heart, amazed to find there is more
than her father allowed: *Oh brave new world!*

-ii-

Late afternoon. The playwright, director,
actors ask me (all legs, all eyes—they call
me *shape*) to join them in the dim theatre,
to share a bottle of pink champagne, a bowl
of ripe strawberries. I hold my breath, can't
wait to tell someone: This is who I am.
I fly downtown on my Mobylette, count
these blessings for my mother. She is calm.
Does she envy the light behind my eyes,
the way my hair falls, the curve of my lip?
Or does she see my father in that glass
of champagne, in my laughter, can't keep
from telling me, *Despite what you may think,*
you're very unattractive when you're drunk.

SNAKE SONG

I dreamt a snake beside the road, thick whip
of licorice stretched in the dusty afternoon,
gloss all smudged by death. I couldn't keep
myself from going back, walking alone
and trying to match the mockingbird
who whistled overhead, while nearby a field
of muddy cattle stood mute and stared,
then suddenly moved to the narrow gate, called
from their grazing by a slant of late
sunlight. I was not afraid. The snake
was dead. I squatted beside him on the hot
tarmac, reached one hand to caress his slack,
scaly length, as a cloud slid across
the sun, and he poured himself into tangled grass.

ADDING IT UP

This is the perfect teatime photograph,
white ruffled tablecloth, red hibiscus
blossoming beside the stone wall. Hands clasped,
my father leans forward, rests his elbows
on bony knees. He's seventy-two, just
two years from dying. My mother crosses
long legs in Bermuda shorts. She's the best
woman singles player at the tennis
club. You'd never guess she was forty-eight.

Perhaps I took this picture. At twenty,
I'm back at home, to be with my father,
trying to catch his eye, to make him stop
looking through me. He sleeps in my small bed.
I sleep in his, across from my mother,
who can't stand his snoring. He no longer
answers when she scolds him, when she pretends
I can't hear her hissing about water
in the gin and how she can't have friends in.

This is the perfect teatime photograph,
white ruffled tablecloth, red hibiscus
blossoming, and my father, who has been
planning this death since before I was born.

SCARECROW

In the dim bedroom, my father stoops,
lays out his clothes for parties
he never plans to attend. Dark blue
pinstriped suit and black suspenders lie

flat across the white bedspread beside
his Christ Church tie, splayed shirt, shined
shoes. My mother isn't fooled. Pushing
the clothes aside, she perches on the edge

of the wide bed to slide her stockings
over slender calves, touches
each seam with a moist fingertip once
before she leaves the house.

SOLACE

When I was fourteen, we moved again,
my mother, in the process, turning
down sea views and verandahs to gain
distance from the bars. The total gain
in the end? Setting all of us down
two miles from town couldn't regain
ground lost years ago—or once again
as she would say. My father's war was long
lost, and the walk far from long
enough to keep him from regaining
a little courage with a small loan
from someone who dealt in loneliness.

And so, when my father lay alone
in the funeral home—once again
we had left him to himself—the lone
viewer was that bartender. The loans
we knew of, we'd paid, and though it turned
out there were others—he alone
knew what was owed, whether one good loan
deserved another, and what marked down
by death—not one of us would go down
when he was there. We left them alone
together. And though we waited a long
time, he never asked. All this was long

ago, but when I learned that our long
time in the womb is far from lonely,
is all natural rapture—this long,
slow spilling of opiate belongs
to the mother (pregnancy's brief gain),
and (to put a dense and very long

treatise in the simplest terms) her long
anticipation gives bliss in turn
to the infant she carries, turning
it dreamily, moving it along
in a sweet drifting around and down
into life, nowhere to go but down—

I thought about my father's walk down
to that bar, saw him choose the longer
way through fields of fennel, pressed down
by his passing, before turning down
behind the oleanders, alone
in sweet shadow and silence, then down
and out into harsh light, and, quick, down
the steps to safety, then back again
into the sun, trying to regain
his balance, shaky when he'd stepped down
from the stool, to make his way home, turn
by turn. I see that walk, that return

whenever I sift the past and turn
up that old photograph of him down
in Bermuda, near the end, head turned,
gin and tonic in one hand, turning
to give the camera a gaze of long,
pure desolation. He had to turn
that grief to stone. How else but turning
back? When we realize we're alone,
I mean, truly understand *alone*—
at the instant of our lover's turn
away from our thin-stretched smile again,
that light shrug when we reach out again—

who hasn't yearned to drown once again
in that sweet, familiar drift and turn,

to taste the rush of solace learned long
before we learned about loneliness,
about our long, slow spiraling down?

CALLING MY FATHER BY NAME

Home for your funeral I wake
before the light to the crack
of a falling blind and call
your name for the last time.
Later that day the sea unfolds
violet and turquoise, hibiscus
blooms scarlet outside the church
window, and I sing *Beloved let us
love,* without missing a beat,

then follow your cedar coffin out
the door and through the rows
of whitewashed graves to a cave
rimmed dark with torn earth, wreathed
bright with flowers. So many, I wonder
to myself, so many, someone important
must have died, and fold my arms
across my chest, close my eyes
against your leaving.

For the next seven years I will hide
your face, hold your name under
my tongue, until the day we fall
from a forgotten book, arm in arm
in color, oleander arching pink
above our solemn smiles. Only
then will the cry break sharp
against my frozen throat,
calling you back, to let me go.

MY FATHER'S GIFT

Hearing of my failure,
my father turned his face
from death for the moment,
and we spent my sixteenth
summer enclosed in screen
and limestone, a porch
high above the harbor,
where he taught me to take
apart those solid blocks
of Latin that scholars love
to call *the unseen*. Head
bent to the book, long fingers
resting on the uneasy
card table, he returned

to his Oxford days, the blithe,
young scholar fifty years gone
by then, handed me the keys
to those blank walls of words,
and we passed through them
together. And so, as the sun
skipped coins of light
on the sea below, and oleander
drifted pink and white
in the corner of my eye,
I learned to love the unseen.

I have lost all my Latin
now, but this morning,
when I opened his Christ
Church notebook, I found
again what he gave me

that summer—set down
in cramped filigree, thirty
years and more before
my birth, the life
of the mind, exuberant,
contained, still blossoming
on the faded page.

WATER DEEPLY

CLOSE TO DARKNESS

VOYAGER

I see you standing, feet apart, your hair
pushed under a peaked cap, your eyes cool, fixed
on the horizon, one hand raised to check
the wind, the other light on the tiller.

Now the sails flap once, twice, and fill, seagulls
stand still on the air, then plunge to circle
your wake, cries echoing those left behind,
and you clear the harbor's mouth, setting out

from the rough island of your birth to sail
around the world, the clamor of the dark
sea for music, the cold stars your only
company. No matter that you never

did it. The gift is the dream, and you telling
me of it in this room, a lifetime later.

MY MOTHER REMEMBERS CLOTHES

Can tell me, fifty years later, what she wore
(burgundy velvet, floor length black cape) the night
she met Goebbels, reached up to open a door

because she was taller. Knows the exact cut
of that pale yellow chiffon (on the bias)
made for the garden party where she forgot

her long gloves and was forced to borrow. Still sees
the silken swirl of pink at her knees, the day
she could have dropped those geraniums (she says)

right onto Hitler's head from a balcony,
just a week before the ambassador found
my father, the two of them on holiday,

and warned them, *Keep going*. Leather bound
books, Queen Anne chairs, Georgian silver, bright
silks, velvets, chiffons, everything left behind

in the British Embassy, to be bombed late
one night, when the Royal Air Force did its best
to level that part of Berlin. Today we sit

in her garden—she holds her hands wrist to wrist
to show the fit, the curve of her slender waist.

MY MOTHER
AND THE BABY'S BREATH

Doomed by my mother's musings,
the lanky gypsophila droops
over her pansies, choking off
the light with a net of tiny
buds. For ten days I fight for it.
Wait until it blooms, I plead,
then decide. But she's not
listening, so one morning, meek
under her direction, I take
the shovel and, while she pulls,
begin to dig out the sprawling plant.

Its roots are huge, like little yams,
like early sweet potatoes, and it puts
up a great fight, but soon she stands
triumphant in the pale June sun,
waving the baby's breath
aloft, its frothy veil spilling
around her head, while all around
her feet, velvet pansies and leggy
petunias raise their faces to the light.

She's right, of course. She always is
about gardening. The secret
she teaches me over and over
is brutality: cutting out the weak,
no matter how beautiful,
pinching back now,
if you want opulence later.

HOMING

Late summer mornings, I deadhead my mother's
garden, pinching the petunia's bruised velvet,
snapping faded stars of nicotiana.
The day before I leave, I gather handfuls

of California poppies for her favorite
vase. She cries when she sees the float of saffron
above the sea-green glass, then tells me again
of her plans for a bed of winter pansies,

and asks me to come with her to the garden
one last time. Holding on to my shoulder, hard,
she bends to pluck a patch of clover, heart-shaped
leaves hiding in clusters of white impatiens.

A week later, kneeling in my neglected
garden, lost in tapestries of burnt orange
marigolds, blue scrawl of cornflowers, I lean
to snap the withered blossoms, pull the lusty

weeds, and an old pain fingers my neck, rocks me
back on my heels to watch the long fall shadows
spill across the lawn, the promise of winter
gathering in, taking them weed and blossom,

one by one.

STUMBLING INTO THE LIGHT

The last of the spring storm snatches
a white skein, scatters it across
washed-out blue, and my daffodils
shrug through the melting snow, pushing
their tight-wrapped buds into the sun.
I'm planning Sunday's phone call, how
I'll describe the way I knelt, touched
the thick, wet clods, and thought about
thumbing seeds into small pockets
of soil—nubbed nasturtium kernels,
pepper sprinkles of snapdragons,
tufted marigold wings—remind
her how much she loved that waiting
for the earth to feather green,
like Lazarus tearing his rotting
grave clothes free, laughing out loud
as he stumbles into the light.

HER DEATH SCENE

"Darling, please call your sister and ask her
to call me before I go away." I wince,
rewind, replay the message until I hear
it right. My mother's talking about Venice,
my sister's long-planned trip, saying "Before

she goes away," slapping me right in the middle
again, not talking about dying, not about to,
and yet at eighty-seven she could have a trick
or two locked inside to haul us out
there, a body-plan hidden in the dark

surge of her blood. I see us beside
her bed, while she makes her exit in style:
my sister, arms folded, face taut
with rage, lips pinching back that hurt smile
she saves for her once-every-three-years visit;

me, as close as I can stand, shuddering the grief
I've been saving, to let my mother believe
I forgive her for never loving anyone, not even
herself. Who knows? Perhaps the three
of us will surprise each other before we shut

down the show at last—my sister dissolving
into racking sobs of remorse, my mother
embracing her daughters' need for love as her own,
while I stand, distracted, inattentive,
and let myself go frozen to the bone.

HER GIFTS

Stand up straight, you stupid bitch, my mother
chides her ninety-year-old bones with offhand
venom, then croons to an extravagant
peony, tilting her head to proffer
her most enchanting smile to a passing
man, before moving on, beaming, nodding,
nudging me in sly delight every time
she drags a response from someone whose mind
and heart are otherwise engaged. These are
her gifts: a passion for the natural
world and an indefatigable charm—
two near perfect disguises for a self-
loathing so inventive, so pervasive,
it never fails to snatch my breath away.

STONE

-i-

Crows haunt the trees, the raucous branches
loud enough to turn my steps right, down
to the shore—that range of blue mountains
cloud-caught across gray water, the slant
of pebbles and sand, now sodden, now hard.
I build my usual shrine—of stones
balanced on driftwood—cap it with green
sea-glass, think of my sister's frozen heart
keeping her home, safe from the push-pull
of love and casual spite that waits
here at our mother's house. Now the waves
chase around my wet shoes, and I fall
back, timing the rhythms of the smooth
rush-retreat of tide, planning my moves.

-ii-

I believe that everyone has inside
them a lonely heart, my mother remarks,
startling me with syntax as she eyes
a man shuffling past our bench. She starts
to speak again, then shrugs, because she's done
with this idea, and gets up to wander
on alone, leaning on her painted cane.
I veer left, down to the beach, and boulder-
step to a stretch of drenched logs, where water
surges, spilling ice across a tumble
of stones. I pick one to bring back to her,
make sure to shift its smooth weight palm to palm
all the way home, keeping it cold as grief,
the way it was when I took it from the sea.

LATELY MY MOTHER

is obsessed with light, prowling the silent
house, the breathing night, crouching, muttering,
transferring plugs from wall to wall, flipping
switches, wailing when she can't jam the prongs

back into sockets, can't flood her bedroom
with light. Sometimes she'll stop, perching the edge
of the bed to weep and rock in the heart
of her fear, until she must start again.

But one blessed night, she tells me, she slid
off smooth sheets and couldn't rise—her nightgown,
her last little slippery silk vanity,
hanging loose on her bones, letting her down

gently, to curl on the rug till morning
called again, and she heard the light singing.

THEY SAY

They say in the months before she died, my mother
roamed the house late at night, babbling and naked,
searching for someone to embrace, while the timid
young care-worker hid and giggled her terror.

They say by day my mother huddled outside the house,
refusing to button her coat against the cold,
that twice the next door neighbor came upon her, wild-
eyed, wearing those pink and yellow plaid sneakers,

with just a half-slip, they say, ribs pushing through thin
gray skin, flesh hanging from her bones, as she bent
to weed her garden, before she rose, turned, and wept—
clawed her face and howled for all she had forgotten.

MY DAUGHTER

imagines getting here
in time, sees herself
sitting beside me
holding my hand, believes
this will make
a difference. What does
she know about dying?

While I am staring
at the mirror
image of this mad
woman I have become,
rushing room
to room to find
the lights, turn them on, off, on,
she is miles away. Her voice, high
and sweet on Sunday mornings,
says *please be who you were,*
but I am already making plans.

Nights I push past
the stupid young woman
paid to care for me
and stand alone outside
for hours. The moonlight
is cold, casting splintered
shadows all around me, the earth
hard underfoot. I need
to learn about coldness, about
darkness, about hardness,
and no one
can bring me inside.

And now that she tells me
she and her sister
are coming, I know
it is time
to find
the darkness
I am dreaming.

FLESH

Good night my darling little baby,
she croons, just before
hanging up the phone.
I stare into the three thousand miles
between this room
and the nursing home bed
where she lies trapped,
her once perfect legs a mass of red
and black bruises, strapped
tight with sticky tape
that will tear her paper
skin off in bloody strips if she lets
herself live long enough
for a change of dressing.

I have long known her fierce need
to be the only beloved,
but just for a moment
I let myself believe
in that murmur,
let myself return
to the sweet, milky darkness
of flesh on flesh,
before she marked me
other, before she saw me
as threat.

DISTRACTION

She fingers the slim gold
barrel of the Cross pen
she found in one
of her mother's purses,
recalls her stepsister
flying in the day after
to begin her brisk
packing and sorting,
stacking sweaters,
shaking out
skirts and blouses,
stuffing limp silk
nightgowns
into garbage bags.

Out loud she chides herself
for things left
undone,
makes promises
she knows she can not
keep, but feels no need
to explain
how she finds herself
distracted by the hibiscus
on her porch,
its ruffled scarlet petals
deepening
to a second glossy flower
at the center,
its stamen tendriled
thick with pollen
just before it opens

into five velvet prongs
at the tip,

and begins
to spend her mornings
sitting and staring
into these bright blossoms,
thinking perhaps
this is all
she needs
to help her remember
nothing
except grief.

GARDENING NOTES: JULY 2003

When I found her gardening notes
sweet peas along fence on south side
I recalled my own plans for that heady
drift of pink and lavender
May: Campanulas
too late for that perennial spill
of pale blue bellflowers
smallest not
tall plants when
get seedlings
by the time I flew home
leggy stars of cosmos
petunias drooping purple velvet
the only ones left
water deeply
close to
darkness
soil cracked and grey with neglect.

But checking the morning glories
I planted the day she died
I find the first blossom
not that unlikely blue promised
on the seed packet
hastily staked in the mud six weeks ago
but white like watered silk
dissolving into pale green
until a breeze lifts
one heart-shaped leaf
to let the sun turn
that cool center
into a thin wash
of yellow light.

Edwina Trentham was born in Bermuda, where she spent the first four years of her life, then moved to Washington DC, where her father was Treasurer of the British Embassy. When she was nine, her father retired and the family returned to Bermuda, where she spent the rest of her childhood. She moved to Connecticut in 1962. She has been a fellow at Yaddo and has published her work in a number of magazines, including *The American Scholar, The American Voice, The Connecticut Review* (forthcoming), *The Massachusetts Review, The New Virginia Review, Prairie Schooner, The Sun,* and *Yankee.* Her work is included in four anthologies—the 1997 *Anthology of Magazine Verse and Yearbook of American Poetry; At Our Core: Women Writing About Power; Atomic Ghost: Poets Respond to the Nuclear Age;* and *By the Long Tidal River: An Anthology of Connecticut Writing* (Curbstone Press, forthcoming). She won honorable mention in the 2004 Sunken Garden Poetry Festival National Competition and has given many readings in New England and New York. Edwina Trentham is a Professor of English at Asnuntuck Community College in Enfield, CT, where she edits the poetry magazine *Freshwater;* and she is also a Visiting Instructor in the Graduate Liberal Studies Program at Wesleyan University. She has one son, Ben, and lives in Guilford with her husband, Greg Coleman, a labyrinth designer, poet, and Tai Chi instructor. They are both members of the Guilford Peace Alliance.

For discussion and writing suggestions
that will add to your enjoyment of
Stumbling into the Light
see the seminar page
of the Antrim House website:
www.antrimhousebooks.com

To order additional copies
of *Stumbling into the Light*
or other Antrim House
titles, visit your local
bookstore or contact
the publisher at

Antrim House
P.O. Box 111
Tariffville, CT 06081
860-217-0023
www.antrimhousebooks.com
eds@antrimhousebooks.com